John Chetham, John Houldsworth

A New and Enlarged Edition of Cheetham's Psalmody

Harmonised in score, with an arrangement for the organ of piano forte

John Chetham, John Houldsworth

A New and Enlarged Edition of Cheetham's Psalmody
Harmonised in score, with an arrangement for the organ of piano forte

ISBN/EAN: 9783744796897

Printed in Europe, USA, Canada, Australia, Japan

Cover: Foto ©Thomas Meinert / pixelio.de

More available books at **www.hansebooks.com**

INSCRIBED TO

THE REVEREND THE VICAR,

And Clergy of the Parish of Halifax.

A NEW AND ENLARGED EDITION

OF

Cheetham's Psalmody,

HARMONIZED IN SCORE;

WITH AN ARRANGEMENT

FOR THE ORGAN OR PIANO-FORTE.

BY

J. HOULDSWORTH,

LATE ORGANIST AT THE PARISH CHURCH, HALIFAX.

"LET EVERY THING THAT HATH BREATH PRAISE THE LORD."—*Psalm c. 6.*

WITH A SUPPLEMENT,

COMPILED, ARRANGED, AND WRITTEN

BY

DR. ROBERTS,

ORGANIST OF MAGDALEN COLLEGE, OXFORD.

LONDON:
MILNER AND COMPANY, LIMITED,
PATERNOSTER ROW.

TO THE REVEREND

THE VICAR AND CLERGY

OF THE PARISH OF HALIFAX,

THIS SELECTION OF SACRED MUSIC,

IS, BY PERMISSION,

MOST RESPECTFULLY INSCRIBED,

BY THEIR

VERY GRATEFUL

AND MOST OBEDIENT SERVANT,

J. HOULDSWORTH.

PREFACE TO THE ORIGINAL EDITION.

ALTHOUGH the appearance of this work has been deferred longer than was anticipated by the Editor, when the design of publication was first announced, it is hoped that the subscribers will not think that they have just cause to complain of the delay when they are informed that it has been occasioned by the extension of the work much beyond the original intention, and by the unwearied pains which have been taken to render it as complete as possible.

The Selection of Tunes, which has been made with great care, contains almost every variety of metre and expression that can be required for sacred poetry. For this purpose, only such Tunes have been taken from the old Editions of Cheetham's Psalmody, as have long maintained their popularity: many other works have been examined, and several valuable Tunes selected from them; but, in making extracts, neither the harmony nor the distribution of parts have been uniformly followed.

The melodies are given according to the most approved copies, in keys best adapted to Congregational Singing; and the Harmonies are arranged with the greatest attention to accuracy and purity.

The Score contains four parts: the Tenor and Alto, from a compliance with custom, are written in the Treble Clef; the harmonist will, therefore, perceive that they appear an octave above their real pitch; and that the Treble or Air, with the harmony for keyed instruments, is placed next to the Bass for the convenience of the performer.

For the parts of the Liturgy designed to be sung, there will be found a great number of Chants, selected from the works of the best masters, and arranged so as to render this style of Music easy of performance.

With a design to promote uniformity, and to assist Choirs who may wish to introduce chanting into the service, words have been set to each kind of Chant, in such a manner that very little application will be required to enable Singers to perform this part of the service with propriety and effect.

Although the Chants in this Work are divided into Classes, as the Te Deums, Jubilates, &c., yet any of them may be exchanged, at the pleasure of the performers, provided that the words are placed according to the examples. With respect to the style in which Chants should be sung, the principal object to be attended to is, a distinct and forcible articulation of the words; the recited part of the verse must occupy no longer time than a good reader would require to pronounce it, and the cadence must be given in correct time, the beating of which can be felt; dwelling upon the first, or any other word, ought to be avoided, as well as hurrying the words in a confused manner; otherwise the proper effect of this simple and appropriate style of Music will be entirely destroyed.

The Response to the Commandments should be sung in a soft and subdued tone of voice, and requires more expression and feeling in the performance than is necessary in Psalm Tunes; but as this impressive part of the singing is generally left to the Choir, it is therefore unnecessary to give any further directions here. The Doxology at the end of the Response must be sung in full chorus.

The Gloria Patris are intended to be sung at the conclusion of the last Psalm for the day, particularly in Churches where the voluntary is not used; and it is scarcely requisite to observe, that they ought to be sung *Con Spirito*.

In forming a Choir of Singers for a Church or Chapel, (either with or without an organ,) the Treble and Bass may be a little predominant; with this exception, the several parts ought to balance as evenly as possible. No singer should attempt to overpower those who accompany him merely because his voice may happen to be a little stronger than theirs; but each person ought to blend his part with the others, that the whole may seem but one full chord of harmony.

In conclusion, this work has been undertaken for the purpose of introducing, into one book, nearly all the best Psalm Tunes, &c., which are regularly sung in this part of the kingdom, along with a few others of the same character, from various places; and if it tend to improve the taste for good Psalmody, and to promote its practice in public and private worship, the Editor will not regret the labour and time which have been devoted to its accomplishment.

PREFACE TO THE SUPPLEMENT.

It is by special request that this Supplement has been written and compiled.

My object has been to add to Cheetham's Psalmody what I deemed would be most useful, and should that object be attained, I shall be much gratified.

The Supplement consists of 29 Psalm Tunes, 90 Single Chants, 22 Double Chants, 9 Kyrie Eleisons, (which are all written in short score,) and the Nicene Creed in monotone, with organ accompaniment.

J. V. ROBERTS.

Formerly Organist & Choir-Master at the Halifax Parish Church.

INDEX TO THE PSALM TUNES.

LONG METRES.

	Page		Page		Page		Page
Birstal	13	Fertile Plains	21	Milton	24	Rockingham	17
Calcott	27	Haydn	19	Montgomery	11	Sabbath New	28
Canada	33	Highbury	36	Mount Moriah	4	Sandbach	40
Cedar	15	Islington	31	New Court	14	Stonefield	29
Clifford's	34	Job	44	Ossett	26	Tranquillity	16
Cork	20	Justification	37	Passing Bell	10	Wainwright	6
Cooke's Morning Hymn	35	Lindley's	32	Paul's, St.	5	Wareham	41
		Litchfield	38	Peter's, St.	23	Warrington	8
Creation	42	Mark's, St.	22	Pontefract	7	Widdop	2
Edwinston	18	Martin, St.	30	Portuguese	12	Windle	3
Evening Hymn	9	Mather's Hymn	25	Psalm 100	1		

COMMON METRES.

	Page		Page		Page		Page
Abridge	77	Cheetham's	92	Langshaw	79	Northgate	78
America	71	Clark's	72	Liverpool	83	Richmond	66
Ann's, St.	45	Croft	56	London, New	51	Shrewsbury	86
Arabia	58	David's, St.	63	London	64	Suffolk	85
Augustine, St.	68	Devizes	59	Luke, St.	54	Trinity	50
Axbridge	48	Devotion	76	Lydia	60	University	57
Bath Chapel	52	Fenwick	74	Manchester	80	Wainwright's 84th	94
Bedford	89	George, St.	73	Mary, St.	61	Warwick	75
Bennett's	65	Halifax	46	Matthew's, St.	96	Wiltshire	49
Bethel	84	Heighington's	67	Melody	82	Windsor, Old	53
Broomsgrove	88	Irish	47	Michael, St.	81	Winchester	70
Burnett	90	James, St.	55	Mount Pleasant	69		
Canterbury	62	John's, St.	87	Naylor's	91		

SHORT METRES.

	Page		Page		Page		Page
Andrew, St.	111	Cranbrook	118	Matthias	113	Pelham	114
Bernard, St.	107	Handel	116	Milton Abbey	108	Sarah	104
Bride's, St.	109	Harrington	106	Mount Ephraim	100	Shirland	99
Cambridge, Old	105	Huddersfield	112	Nares	110	Stow	117
Christianity	102	Mather's Morning Hymn	98	Peckham	101	Watchman	103

PECULIAR METRES.

	Page		Page		Page		Page
Advent	152	Christmas Hymn	153	Handel's 104th	142	Narcissus	121
Arne's	136	Dismission	138	Helen's, St.	129	Pleyel's Hymn	120
Ascension	140	Easter Hymn	143	Helmsley	145	Portsmouth	126
Baxter	158	Eaton	128	Hotham	122	Queenborough	150
Burnham	132	Goshen	156	Luther's Hymn	146	Sabbath, Old	141
Calvary	149	Grosvenor	159	Lynn	125	Vesper Hymn	148
Canaan	160	Haydn's German Hymn	157	Mariner's Hymn	124	Warsaw	144
Carey's	134			Mawdsley Street	154	Whitby	130

INDEX TO THE CHANTS, &c.

	Page	Page		Page	Page
Te Deum	162 to	169	Magnificat	199 —	201
Benedicite and Benedictus	170 —	171	Deus Misereatur	202 —	204
Jubilate	172 —	179	Responses	205 —	220
Cantate	180 —	189	Gloria Patri	221 —	229
Nunc Dimittis	190 —	198	Collect		230

INDEX TO THE SUPPLEMENT.

PSALM TUNES.

	Page
Angel's Hymn, L.M	245
Augustine, S.M.	246
Batavia, P.M.	243
Carlisle, S.M.	235
Christ Church, P.M.	236
Crasselius, L.M.	233
Dix, P.M.	242
Dundee, C.M.	234
Eventide, P.M.	247
Farrant, C.M.	246
Franconia, S.M.	234
Hall, P.M.	235
"I Could not Do Without Thee." P.M.	238
Jersey, P.M.	243
Keble, P.M.	247
Lubeck, P.M.	241
Melcombe, L.M.	233
Merton, P.M.	236
Sherbourne, P.M.	241
S. Michael, S.M.	237
S. Theodulph, P.M.	240
St. Peter, C.M.	234
Swabia, S.M.	245
Tallis, C.M.	244
"Thou Art Coming, O my Saviour." P.M.	239
Toulon, P.M	244
Vienna, P.M.	242
"Weary of Earth," P.M.	237
Weber, P.M.	240

	Page	Page
Single Chants	248 to	270
Double Chants	271 —	281
Kyrie Eleisons	282 —	285
The Nicene Creed in Monotone		286

A SHORT

INTRODUCTION TO THE ART OF SINGING.

THE Notes in Music are seven in number, and are named A, B, C, D, E, F, G. They are usually written on five lines, thus, 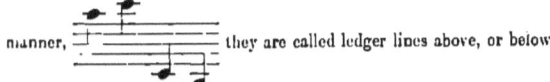 and in the four spaces between the lines, thus,

These lines and spaces form what is termed a Stave; and if there be extra lines at the top or bottom, in this manner, they are called ledger lines above, or below.

In writing the letters in the Treble Clef, C is placed on the first ledger line below, D below the stave, E on the first line, F on the first space, and so on : always advancing from the bottom upwards.

EXAMPLE OF THE LETTERS IN THE TREBLE CLEF.

EXAMPLE OF THE LETTERS IN THE BASS CLEF.

Every Note higher than F on the fifth line in the Treble, is said to be in alt, as G in alt, A in alt, &c. . and every Note lower than G on the first line in the Bass, is called double, as double F, double E, double D, &c.

CLEFS.

There are three Clefs, placed thus, the Treble or G Clef, on the second line; the Bass or F Clef, on the fourth line; and the C Clef sometimes on one line and sometimes on another, and which properly belongs to the Alto and Tenor parts; but to give a general idea of the various Clefs, the following Scales are inserted.

It may not be improper to observe here, that the Treble Clef is now frequently substituted for the C Clef, in the Alto and Tenor parts: and, as it is stationary and less perplexing to the Performer than a fluctuating Clef, it has been adopted throughout the following work.

THE DIFFERENT SORTS OF NOTES AND THEIR PROPORTIONS.

A Dot placed after any Note makes it longer by one half.

Thus, a dotted Semibreve is equal to three Minims; a dotted Minim is equal to three Crotchets, &c.

MUSICAL CHARACTERS.

Each Note is sometimes represented by a Rest, to denote a silence equal in duration to the Note to which it belongs; thus—

A Sharp ♯ placed at the beginning of a piece of Music, on any line or space, shows that all the Notes on that line or space are to be sung half a tone higher than the natural Note.

A Flat ♭ is the reverse of this, and intimates that the Notes to which it refers are to be sung half a tone lower than the natural Note.

A Natural ♮ placed before any Note contradicts the Sharp or Flat, and restores the Note to its natural sound.

Accidental Sharps, Flats, or Naturals, are those which are placed before Notes in the course of a Tune, and only continue through the bar in which they occur.

A Pause ⌢ shows that the Note or Rest over which it is placed may be held rather longer than its proper time.

When three Notes are tied together with the figure 3 over them, thus, they are called a Triplet, and are to be sung in the same time that two of the same character require.

A Tie, or Slur over two or more Notes, directs that they are to be sung to one Syllable.

A single Bar divides the Time into equal portions, according to its measure.

A double Bar divides the parts of a Tune; and when dotted on each side, thus, it denotes that each part is to be sung twice over, and this mark 𝄋 also directs the performer to repeat the part where it is placed.

A small Dash over Notes, thus, signifies that they are to be sung short and detached.

belongs to the Alto and Tenor parts; but to give a general idea of the various Clefs, the following Scales are inserted.

It may not be improper to observe here, that the Treble Clef is now frequently substituted for the C Clef, in the Alto and Tenor parts; and, as it is stationary and less perplexing to the Performer than a fluctuating Clef, it has been adopted throughout the following work.

THE DIFFERENT SORTS OF NOTES AND THEIR PROPORTIONS.

A Dot placed after any Note makes it longer by one half.

Thus, a dotted Semibreve is equal to three Minims; a dotted Minim is equal to three Crotchets, &c.

MUSICAL CHARACTERS.

Each Note is sometimes represented by a Rest, to denote a silence equal in duration to the Note to which it belongs; thus—

A Sharp ♯ placed at the beginning of a piece of Music, on any line or space, shows that all the Notes on that line or space are to be sung half a tone higher than the natural Note.

A Flat ♭ is the reverse of this, and intimates that the Notes to which it refers are to be sung half a tone lower than the natural Note.

A Natural ♮ placed before any Note contradicts the Sharp or Flat, and restores the Note to its natural sound.

Accidental Sharps, Flats, or Naturals, are those which are placed before Notes in the course of a Tune, and only continue through the bar in which they occur.

A Pause ⌢ shows that the Note or Rest over which it is placed may be held rather longer than its proper time.

When three Notes are tied together with the figure 3 over them, thus, they are called a Triplet, and are to be sung in the same time that two of the same character require.

A Tie, or Slur over two or more Notes, directs that they are to be sung to one Syllable.

A single Bar divides the Time into equal portions, according to its measure.

A double Bar divides the parts of a Tune; and when dotted on each side, thus, it denotes that each part is to be sung twice over, and this mark :𝄋 also directs the performer to repeat the part where it is placed.

A small Dash over Notes, thus, signifies that they are to be sung short and detached.

Crescendo < intimates that the sound must be increased—Diminuendo > decreased: and when both are used, thus, <> the Note or Passage is to be begun soft, gradually increasing to loud, and then diminishing to its previous softness.

In the Major Key the Shake must be used on a whole Tone except upon the Third of the chord. In the Minor Key the Shake may be regulated by the Note above in the Scale.

It is not to be supposed, in learning this embellishment, that it can be acquired at once; but it must be practised for a considerable time, in a slow and distinct manner, a little more emphasis being laid on the lower than on the higher Note.

TIME.

There are three sorts of Time, viz. Common, Triple, and Compound or mixed Time; each of which is distinguished by marks or figures: Common Time is marked ₵ ₵ which signifies to the value of four Crotchets in each Bar; the first mark is rather slow, as Andante, the latter quicker, as Allegro. The time expressed by the figures 2/4 is called French Common Time, and contains two Crotchets in each bar.

The figures for Triple Time are 3/2, 3/4, 3/8, which intimates that there are three Minims, three Crotchets, and three Quavers, in a Bar.

The different sorts of Compound Time are expressed by 6/4, 6/8, 9/4, 9/8, 12/8 but these are not much used in Modern Music.

The above figures refer to the Semibreve, which is the standard of reckoning; the lower figure, which is generally 2, 4, or 8, shows into what parts the Semibreve is divided, viz. Minims, Crotchets, or Quavers, and the upper figure denotes how many of those parts make a Bar; thus, in 2/4 the 4 indicates that the Semibreve is divided into four parts or Crotchets, and the 2 that the Bar contains two of those parts, &c.

THE DIATONIC SCALE.

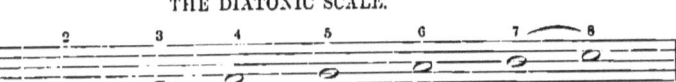

THE CHROMATIC SCALE.

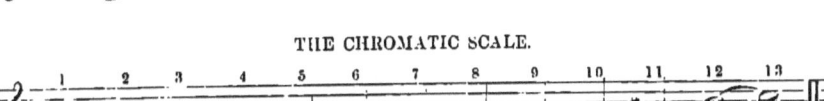

The Diatonic Scale consists of seven sounds, and an eighth which is merely a repetition of the first; the sounds are disposed at intervals of tones and half-tones, the half-tones occur between the 3rd and 4th, and 7th and 8th.

The Chromatic Scale consists of twelve sounds and a repetition of the first; each sound in this scale can be taken as a Key Note, or the beginning of a Diatonic Scale, showing that there are twelve Major Keys; and as each Major Key has what is termed a relative Minor Key, the result will be twenty-four Keys in Music.

EX. OF THE DIFFERENT KEY NOTES, MAJOR AND MINOR.

EX. OF INTERVALS.

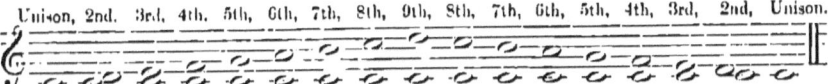

Intervals in the Key of A Minor.

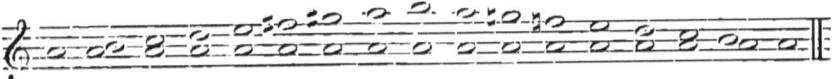

An interval is the distance between any two Notes, ascending or descending. In the Major Key the Notes are all natural; but as the Minor Key is in itself imperfect, an accidental Sharp is usually placed before the 6th and 7th in the ascending Scale; but in descending it is generally taken off, especially in Vocal Music. A proper close or cadence, however, cannot be effected unless a Sharp be placed to the 7th.

A Tune or Piece is in a Major Key, if the distance from the Key Note to the 3rd above consist of five Semitones, as from C to E; but if it consist of only four Semitones, as from A to C, it is in a Minor Key. In all regular Movements or Tunes, the Bass ends upon the Key Note.

SOLMIZATION, OR SOL-FA-ING.

It is now about 800 years since Guido Aretine, a Monk of the Order of St. Benedict, invented the use of certain syllables to teach the practice of Singing; this system having been found much superior to the method then in use was generally adopted throughout Italy. The syllables he made use of, viz., UT, RE, MI, FA, SOL, LA, were taken from a Latin Hymn still extant, composed in honour of John the Baptist.

Lemaire, a celebrated French Musician of the 16th Century, greatly improved upon Aretine's method, and added a seventh syllable, SI, to the before-mentioned six; this plan is still commonly followed in France.

In some of the English publications on this subject, the syllables have been repeated in this manner, FA, SOL, LA, FA, SOL, LA, MI; but the modern Italian method, from its superiority, has now almost superseded all others. This system dismisses the UT and substitutes the more musical intonation DO, and places the seven syllables to the Scale, thus,—

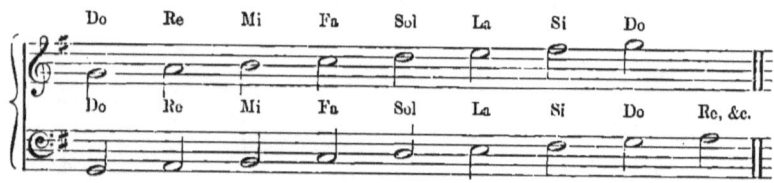

It must be observed that DO is always placed to the Key Note, or the first of the Scale, RE to the second, MI to the third, FA to the fourth, SOL to the fifth, LA to the sixth, and SI to the seventh; the eighth being but a repetition of the first Note, DO is again used, and all the others in the same order of succession, thus showing that every 8th Note, either ascending or descending, is the same in name as well as sound, only more acute or grave according to its situation.

* The Vowels in these syllables are pronounced as in the Italian language, viz., *a* as in father; *e* as the *a* in paper; and *i* as the *e* in me.

XV

EXERCISES IN THE KEY OF C MAJOR.

The above Exercises ought to be practised in various Keys, which may easily be done by copying them, and commencing on a different Key Note, always bearing in mind that DO is the first in the Scale. Any lengthened Examples here would extend this part of the Work beyond the limits proposed.

CADENZA.

Cadenza is an extemporaneous Passage, which a Singer or Solo Performer introduces in a Piece of Music, on the first Note of a final Cadence.—The Cadenza should only be attempted by a Performer who has sufficient knowledge of harmony to introduce one suitable to the style and character of the Piece.

ON ACCENT.

Music is divided into Bars, not only to measure the Time, but also to mark the Notes upon which the Accent is to be laid. Accented Notes are those which require a greater stress than the rest, by which expression is given to the whole: and unless attention be paid to this, however exactly a Piece of Music may be performed, it will have a monotonous sound.

In every Bar of Common Time, which consists of four parts, the first and third are accented, the second and fourth unaccented. In Triple Time of three parts in a Bar, the first only is accented, the second and third unaccented, but the third should be rather stronger than the second. When $\frac{3}{8}$ Time is divided into Quavers, the Accent falls on the first, third, and fifth parts of the Bar: but in $\frac{6}{8}$ Time the first and fourth only are accented.

Sometimes, to produce effect, the Composer places the Accent on the unaccented part of the Bar: this deviation from the rules of Accent is called Emphasis. It is expressed by this mark $>$ under or over a Note, or by *rf*, *fz*.

DIRECTIONS FOR PRACTICE.

To acquire a good and firm tone of voice, let the mouth be opened about a quarter of an inch, and avoid, as much as possible, closing the teeth, or the tongue touching them.

The Scale is the first Lesson, each Note of which ought to be held for a considerable time, beginning soft and increasing till loud, and then diminishing it.

All distortion of the countenance must be avoided, as well as singing through the nose, or too much in the head, as the tone ought to come freely from the chest; and the greatest nicety should be observed, to have the voice perfectly in tune with the Teacher's, or with some well-tuned instrument. Attention to this will not only render the Learner's first attempts at singing more agreeable to others, but will materially improve his own ear for proper sounds. To manage the breath well, it should be taken without noise, and only at proper intervals; as where a rest occurs; after a staccato note (if not dividing a word); after a semibreve or minim, where it is not tied to the next note, and in that case, after the tie; sometimes after a dotted note, but never in the middle of a word.

Attend particularly to the distinct articulation of the words; read them over carefully several times before singing, and let the pronunciation be according to the most correct and approved method.

LONG METRES.

No. 1. THE HUNDREDTH PSALM. L.M. LUTHER.

No. 2. WIDDOP. L.M.

WIDDOP.

Who shall as-cend thy heav'n-ly place, Great God, and dwell be-fore thy face? The man who minds re-li-gion now, And hum-bly walks with God be-low.

No. 5. SAINT PAUL'S. L.M. GREEN.

Thrice hap - py man who fears the Lord, Loves his com -

- mands, and trusts his word! Hon - our and peace his

days at - tend, And bless - ings to his seed de - scend.

No. 6. WAINWRIGHT. L.M.

WAINWRIGHT.

He reigns! the Lord, the Saviour reigns! Praise Him in e-van-gel-ic strains! Praise Him in e-van-gel-ic strains! Let the whole earth in songs rejoice, And distant islands join their voice, And distant islands join their voice.

No. 7. PONTEFRACT. L.M.

No. 10. PASSING BELL. L.M. WHITAKER.

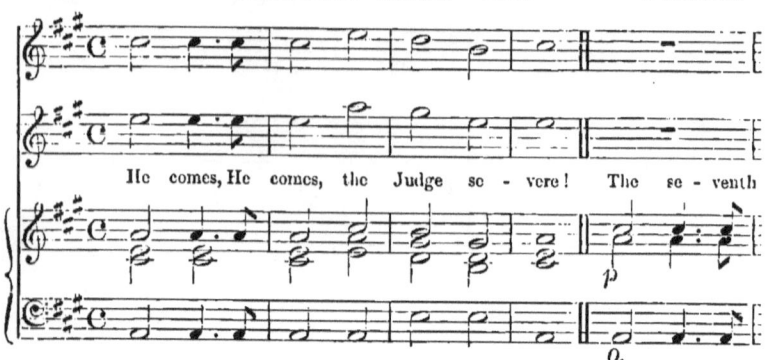

No. 18. EDWINSTON. L.M.

Je - sus shall reign where -'er the sun Does his suc - ces - sive

jour - nies run; His kingdom stretch from shore to shore, Till moons shall

wax and wane no more, Till moons shall wax and wane no more.

No. 19. HAYDN. L.M.

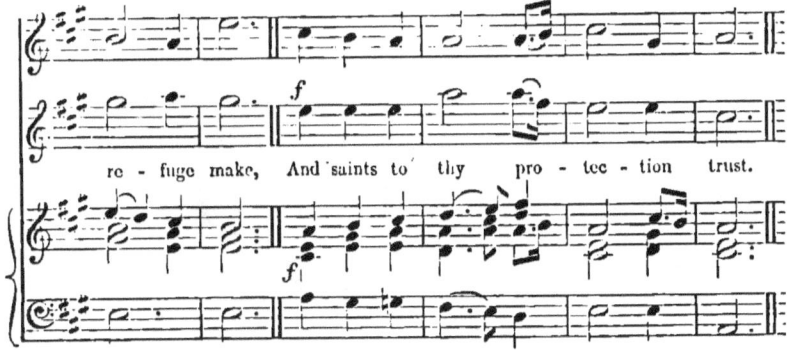

No. 24. MILTON. L.M. Stanley.

Give thanks to God, He reigns a - bove; Kind are his thoughts, his name is Love; His mer - cy a - ges past have known, And a - ges long to come shall own.

No. 25. MATHER'S HYMN. L.M.

No. 29. STONEFIELD. L.M.

No. 31.   ISLINGTON. L.M.

No. 33. CANADA. L.M.

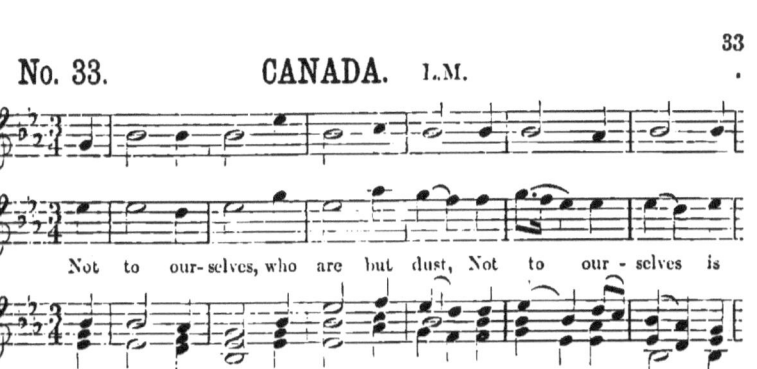

Not to our-selves, who are but dust, Not to our-selves is

glo - ry due, E - ter-nal God, Thou on - ly just, Thou on - ly

gra-cious, wise, and true, Thou on - ly gra - cious, wise, and true.

No. 35. COOK'S MORNING HYMN. L.M.

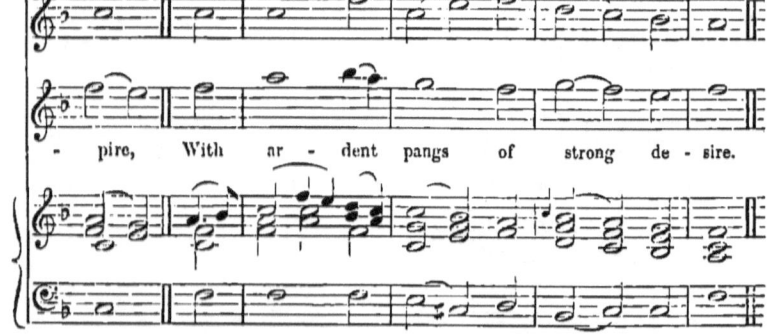

No. 37. JUSTIFICATION. L.M.

No. 39. SANDBACH. L.M.

Come, dear-est Lord, de-scend and dwell By faith and love in ev-'ry breast; Then shall we know, and taste, and feel, The joys that can-not be......... ex-press'd.

No. 40. WAREHAM. L.M.

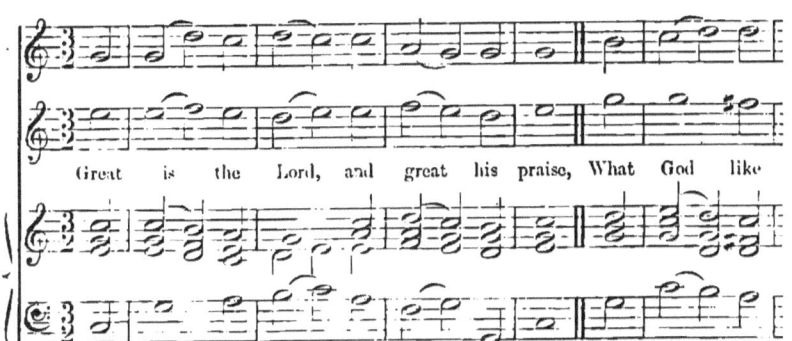

Great is the Lord, and great his praise, What God like

Him our fears can raise; Let ev-'ry peo-ple, ev-'ry

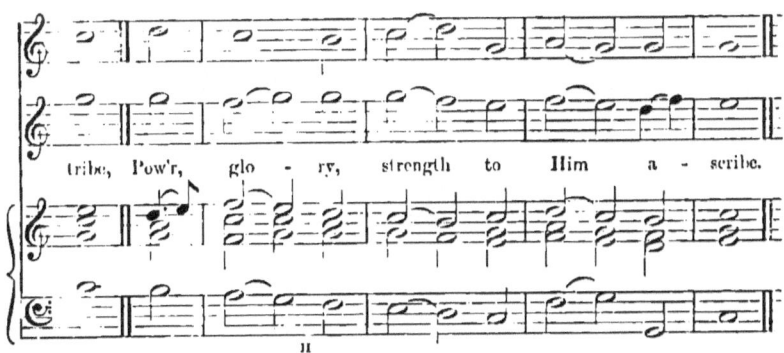

tribe, Pow'r, glo - ry, strength to Him a - scribe.

No. 41. CREATION. L.M. HAYDN.

The spa-cious fir-ma-ment on high, With all the

blue e-the-real sky, And span-gled heav'ns, a

shin-ing frame, Their great o-ri-gi-nal pro-claim.

COMMON METRES.

No. 43. **ST. ANN'S.** Croft.

Through all the chang-ing scenes of life,
In trou-ble and in joy,
The praises of my God shall still,
My heart and tongue em-ploy.

No. 44. HALIFAX. C.M. Widdop.

My lot is fall'n in that blest land, Where God is tru - - ly known; He fills my cup with lib - 'ral hand, He makes his word my own.

No. 47.   WILTSHIRE.   C.M.

No. 49.   NEW LONDON. C.M.

No. 50. BATH CHAPEL. C.M.

No. 52. ST. LUKE. C.M.

Re - mark, my soul, the nar - - row bounds
Of the re - volv - ing year! How swift the weeks complete their rounds, How short the months ap - pear!

No. 55. UNIVERSITY. C.M. HARWOOD.

How sweet the name of Je - sus sounds In a be - - lie - ver's ear! It soothes his sor - rows, heals his wounds, And drives a - way his fear.

No. 56. ARABIA. C.M.

No. 62. LONDON. C.M. CROFT.

Lord, hear my pray'r, and to my cry
Thy wont-ed au-dience lend; In thy ac-cus-tom'd
faith and truth A gra-cious an-swer send.

No. 63.   BENNETS.   C.M.   BENNET.

My God, the spring of all my joys, The life of my de - - lights; The glo - ry of my bright - est days, And com - fort of my nights, And comfort of my nights.

No. 64.   RICHMOND. C.M.

Oh, how I love thy ho - ly law! 'Tis dai - ly my de - light, And thence my me - di - ta - tions draw Di - vine ad - vice by night.

72

No. 70.   **CLARKE'S.**   C.M.

My Shep-herd is the liv-ing Lord, I there-fore no-thing need; In pas-tures fair,... near plea-sant streams, He setteth me to feed,... *f* set-teth me to feed, He set-teth me to feed.

No. 71. ST. GEORGE. C.M.

74

No. 72. FENWICK. C.M.

Plung'd in a gulf of dark de-spair,
We wretch-ed sin-ners lay; With-out one cheer-ing
beam of hope, Or spark of glim-m'ring day.

No. 76. NORTHGATE. C.M.

In - struct me in thy sta - tutes, Lord, Thy right - eous paths dis - play; That I from them, through all my life, No more may go a - stray.

No. 77. LANGSHAW. C.M.

O for a heart to praise my God, A heart from guilt set free; A heart that's sprin-kled with the blood So free-ly shed for me.

No. 79. ST. MICHAEL. C.M. WAINWRIGHT.

Come, Ho - ly Spi - rit, God of might.

The com - fort - er of all; Teach us to know thy

word a - right, That we may ne - ver fall.

No. 83.   SUFFOLK. C.M.

No. 87. BEDFORD. C.M. COOMBS.

Dread Sov - 'reign! let my eve - ning song
Like ho - ly in - cense rise; As - sist the off - 'rings
of my tongue To reach the lof - ty skies.

No. 90. CHEETHAM'S. C.M.D.

How vast must their ad-van-tage be, How great their plea-sure prove, Who live like bre-thren, and con-sent In of-fi-ces of love.

SHORT METRES.

No. 93. MATHER'S MORNING HYMN.

No. 94.   SHIRLAND.   S.M.   Stanley.

Come, Ho - ly Spi - rit, come, Let thy bright beams a - - rise; Dis - pel the dark - ness from our minds, And o - - - pen all our eyes.

No. 97. CHRISTIANITY. S.M.

No. 98.   WATCHMAN. S.M.   LEACH.

To God, the on - ly wise, Our Sa - viour

and our King, Let all the Saints be -

- low the skies Their hum - ble prai - ses sing.

No. 99.   SARAH.   S.M.

No. 100. OLD CAMBRIDGE. S.M. HARRISON.

To bless thy cho - sen race, In mer - cy, Lord, in - cline; And cause the bright - ness of thy face On all thy Saints to shine.

No. 101.   HARRINGTON. S.M.

No. 104. ST. BRIDE'S. S.M.

No. 106.   ST. ANDREW.   S.M.

God will con-found them all, Who do op-pose his will; They shall be turn-ed back and fall, That wish his peo - - ple ill.

No. 109.   **PELHAM.**   S.M.

With hum-ble heart and tongue, My God, to Thee I pray; O make me learn, while I am young, How I may cleanse my way. Now in my

No. 115. **HOTHAM.** Eight 7s.

No. 116. MARINER'S HYMN. Four 7s.

No. 118. PORTSMOUTH. 4 6. 2-8.

Ye bound-less realms of joy, Ex - alt your Ma - ker's fame; His praise your songs em - ploy,........ A - bove the star-ry frame,........ His praise your songs em - ploy, A - bove the star-ry

No. 123. CAREY'S. Six 8s.

136

No. 124. **ARNE'S.** Six 8s.

Hap - py the man whose hopes re - ly On
Is - rael's God; He made the sky, And
earth, and sea, with all their train; His

No. 125. **DISMISSION.** 4-S. 4-7. From the Missal.

Come, Thou long ex-pect-ed Je-sus, Born to set thy peo-ple free; From our fears and sins re- lease us, Let us find our rest in Thee. Is - rael's

140

No. 126.   **ASCENSION.** 4-6. 2-8.   Matthews.

Join all the glo - rious names Of wis - dom, love, and pow'r,

That ev - er mor - tals knew, That an - gels ev - er bore,

All are too mean to speak his worth, Too mean to set my Sa - viour forth.

No. 127. OLD SABBATH. Four 10s.

A - gain the day re-turns of ho-ly rest, Which, when He made the world, Je-hovah blest, When like his own, He bade our labours cease, And all be pi-e-ty and all be peace, And all be pi-e-ty and all be peace.

No. 129.   EASTER HYMN.   P.M.

No. 132. LUTHER'S HYMN. P.M.

150

No. 135. QUEENBOROUGH. 4-8s. 4-7s.

No. 136.   **ADVENT.**   3-8. 3-7

Lo! He comes, with clouds descending, Once for favour'd sinners slain,

Thousand, thousand saints attending, Swell the triumphs of his train;

Hallelujah! Hallelujah! Jesus now shall ever reign.

No. 138. **MAWDSLEY STREET.** 4-8, 2-6.

No. 139.   **GOSHEN.** Four 8s.

In-spir-er and hear-er of pray'r, Thou shep-herd and guar-dian of thine; My all to thy co-ve-nant care, I sleep-ing or wak-ing re-sign.

No. 140. HAYDN'S GERMAN HYMN. 4-8s. 4-7s.

161

End of the Psalm Tunes.

CHANTS.

No. 1.   TE DEUM.   JACKSON.

We praise..Thee O God

To Thee all Angels ....cry   a - - loud
Holy ....Ho - ly   Holy
The glorious company .... of   the   Apostles
The noble .... army   of   martyrs
The..Father
Thou art the......................................King   of   Glory
When Thou tookest upon Thee to de - li - ver   Man
Thou sittest at the right......................hand   of   God
We therefore pray Thee........................ help   thy   servants
O Lord.. save   thy   people
Day .... by   day
Vouch   -   -   -   -   -   -   safe   O   Lord
O Lord let thy mercy...........................lighten up - - on us

We acknowledge.....................Thee   to   be   the   Lord

The Heavens and .... all   the   pow'rs there - in
Lord .... God   of   Sa - ba - oth
Praise..Thee
Praise..Thee
Of an............................... in - finite Ma - jes - ty
O..Christ
Thou didst not ab   -   -   hor   the   Vir - gin's   womb
In the................................glo - ry   of   the   Father
Whom Thou hast redeemed......with   thy   pre - cious   blood
And .... bless thine he - ri - tage
We .... mag   -   -   ni - fy Thee
To keep us .... this   day   with - out   sin
As.................................... our   trust is   in   Thee

No. 2.   TE DEUM.   Robinson.

No. 3.   TE DEUM.   Houldsworth.

No. 4.   TE DEUM.   Attwood.

No. 5. TE DEUM. STEVENSON.

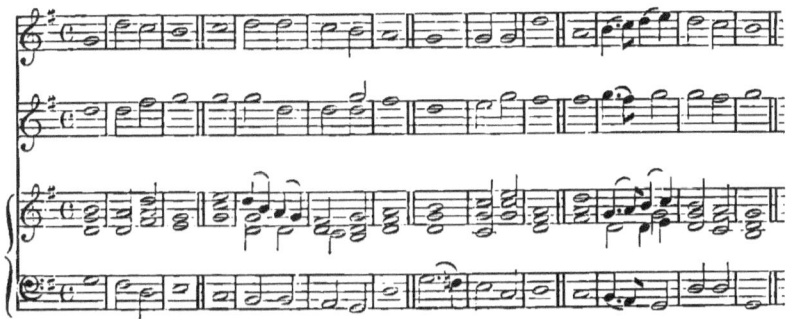

No. 6. TE DEUM. DR. CAMIDGE.

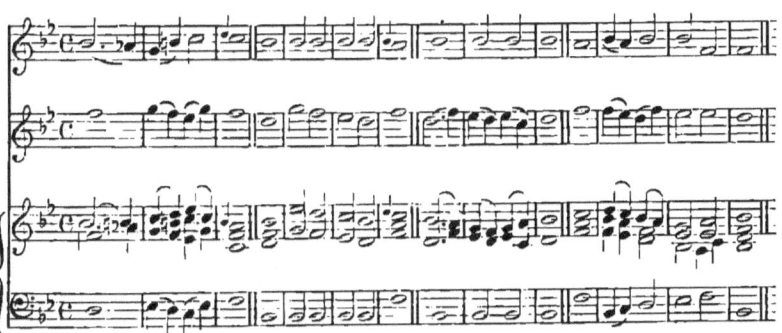

No. 7. TE DEUM.

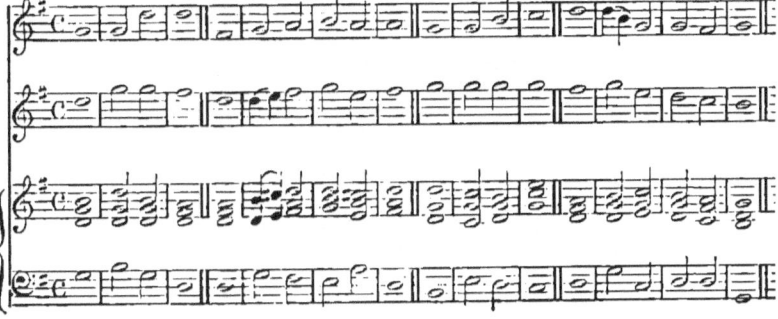

No. 11.   TE DEUM. Corfe.

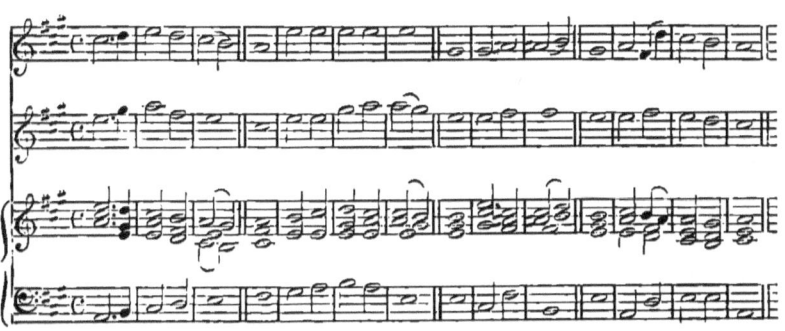

No. 12.   TE DEUM. Houldsworth.

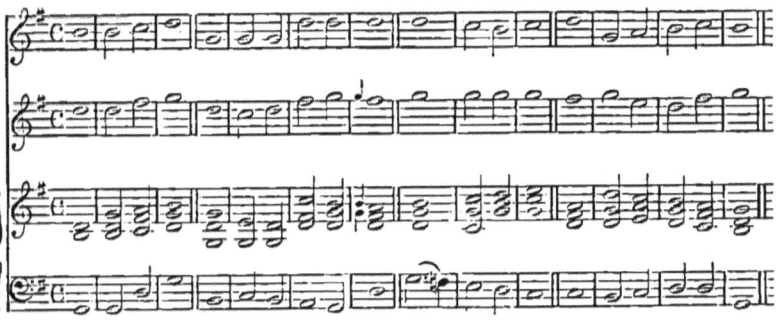

No. 13.   TE DEUM. Hartley.

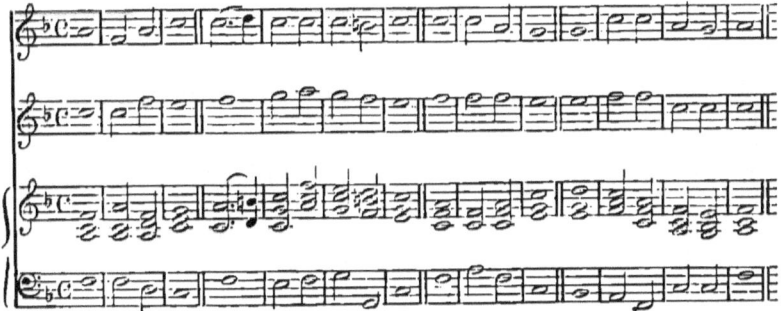

No. 14. TE DEUM. JACKSON.

No. 15. TE DEUM. LANGDON.

No. 16. TE DEUM. DR CROTCH.

No. 17.   TE DEUM.   HOULDSWORTH.

No. 18.   TE DEUM.   *Quadruple Chant.*

No. 24. JUBILATE. Houldsworth.

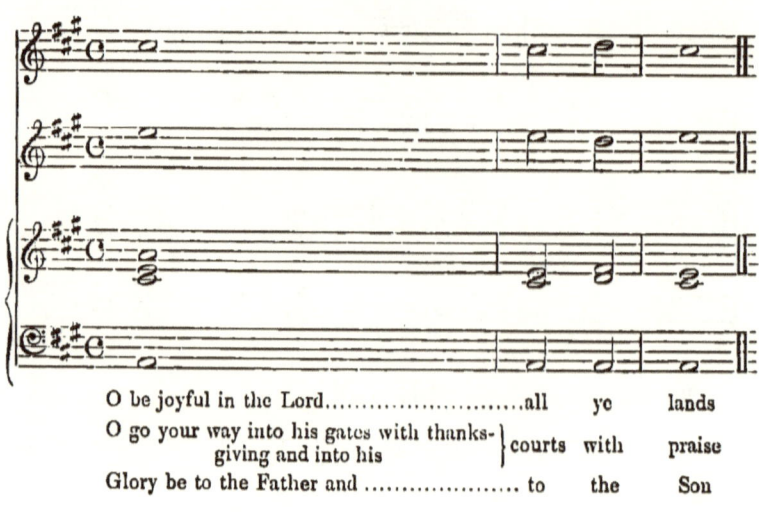

O be joyful in the Lord............................all ye lands
O go your way into his gates with thanks- } courts with praise
giving and into his
Glory be to the Father and .... to the Son

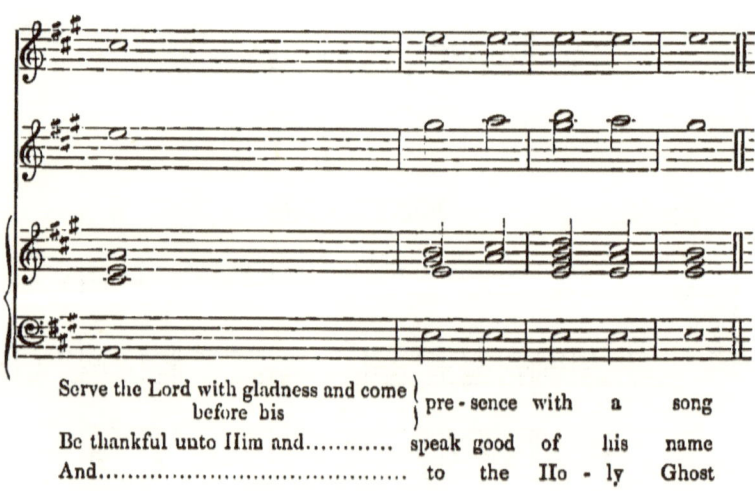

Serve the Lord with gladness and come } pre-sence with a song
before his
Be thankful unto Him and............. speak good of his name
And.. to the Ho-ly Ghost

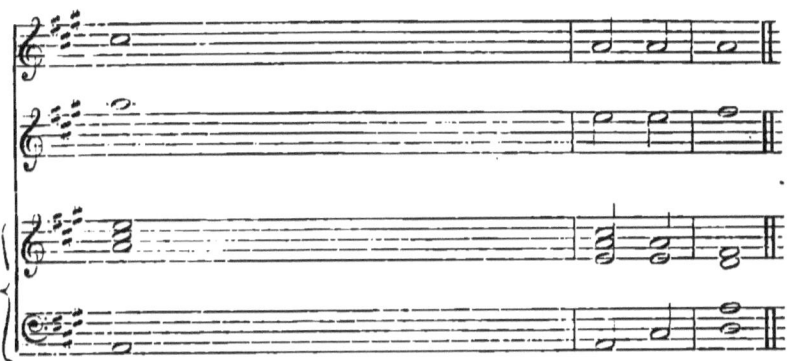

Be ye sure that the Lord He is God : it is He that hath made us and not ... we our - selves
For the Lord is gracious his mercy is.....................e - ver - lasting
As it was in the beginning is now and..................ever shall be

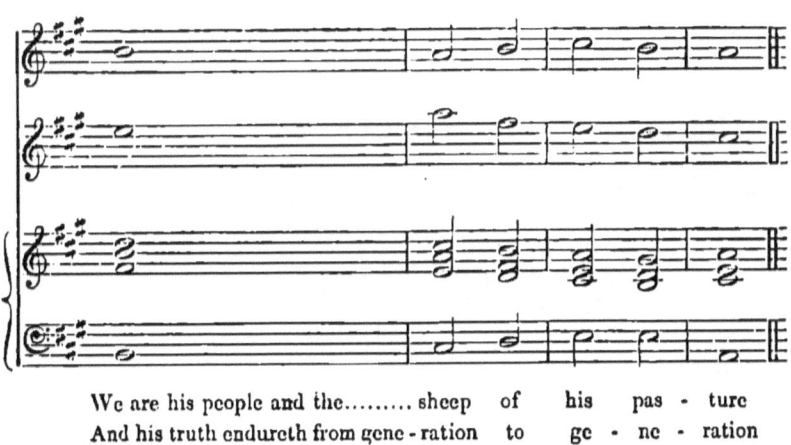

We are his people and the.........sheep of his pas - ture
And his truth endureth from gene - ration to ge - ne - ration
World.............................with - out end A - men.

No. 25.   JUBILATE.   Soaper.

No. 26.   JUBILATE.   Pratt.

No. 27.   JUBILATE.

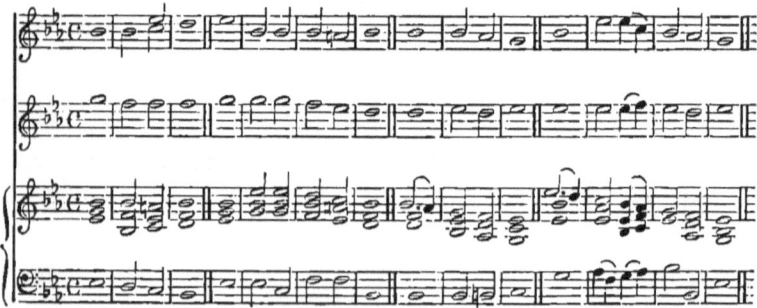

No. 28.   JUBILATE.

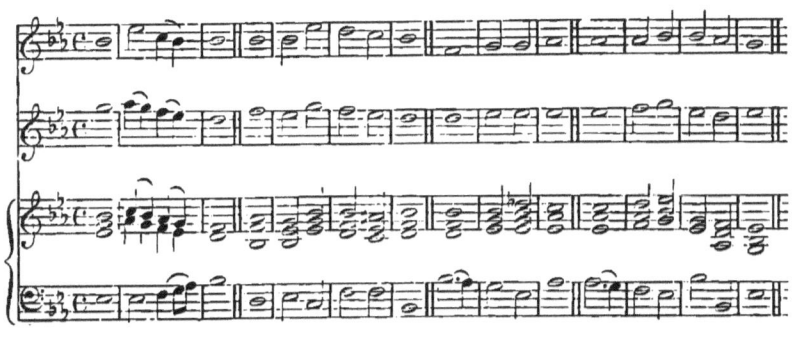

No. 29.   JUBILATE.   KEMP.

No. 30.   JUBILATE.   NARES.

No. 31.   JUBILATE.   WAINWRIGHT.

No. 32.   JUBILATE.   WIDDOP.

No. 33.   JUBILATE.   RUSSELL.

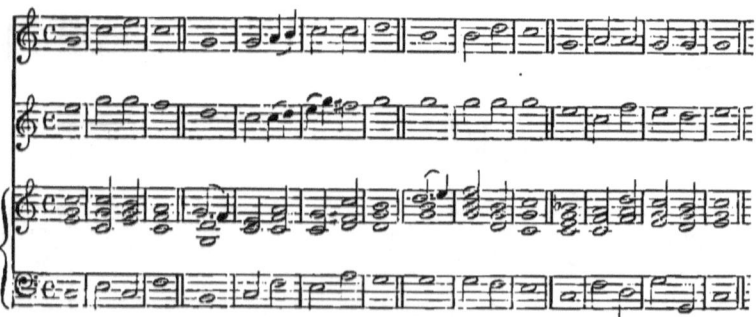

No. 34.   JUBILATE.   Bellamy.

No. 35.   JUBILATE.   Houldsworth.

No. 36.   JUBILATE.   Houldsworth.

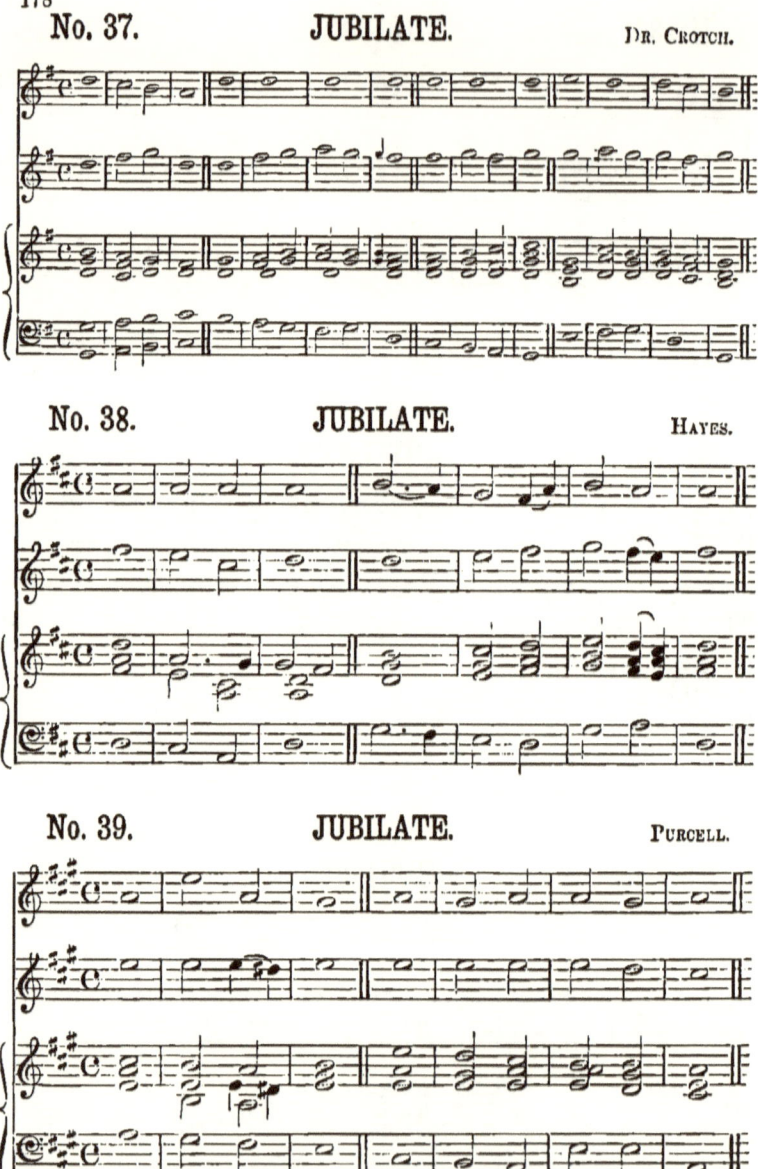

No. 40.   JUBILATE.   HEATHCOTE.

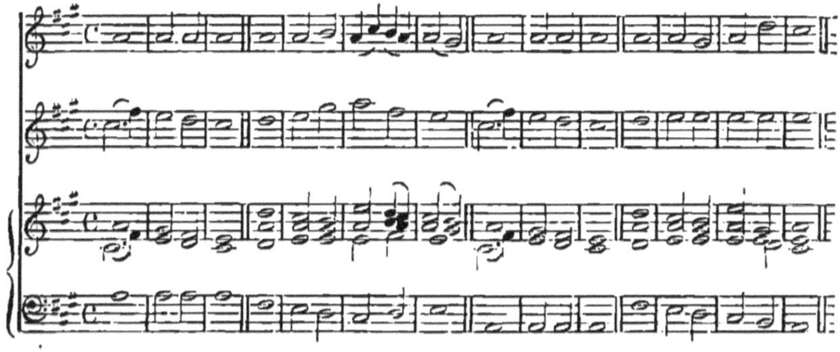

No. 41.   JUBILATE.   WRENSHALL.

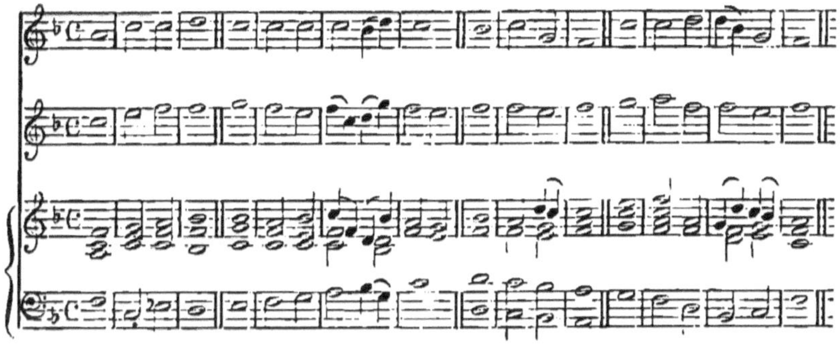

No. 42.   JUBILATE.   BELLAMY.

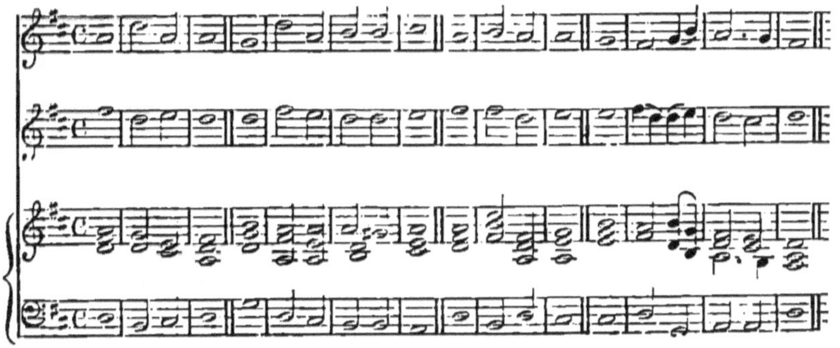

No. 43. CANTATE.
Mornington.

O sing unto the Lord.. a new song
The Lord declared .... his sal - va-tion
Show yourselves joyful unto the Lord .... all ye lands
With trumpets .... also and shawms
Let the floods clap their hands and let the hills be }
                joyful together be - - - } fore the Lord
Glory be to the Father and .... to the Son

For He hath .... done mar-vel-lous things
His righteousness hath He openly showed in the sight of the hea - then
Sing .... re - joice and give thanks
O show yourselves joyful be - - - fore the Lord the King
For He .... cometh to judge the earth
And.. to the Ho - ly Ghost

With his own right hand and with his .... ho - ly   arm
He hath remembered his mercy and truth toward the house of   Israel
Praise the Lord up   -   -   -   -   -   -   on the   harp
Let the sea make a noise and all that..................... there-in   is
With righteousness shall He............................ judge the   world
As it was in the beginning is now and .... ever shall   be

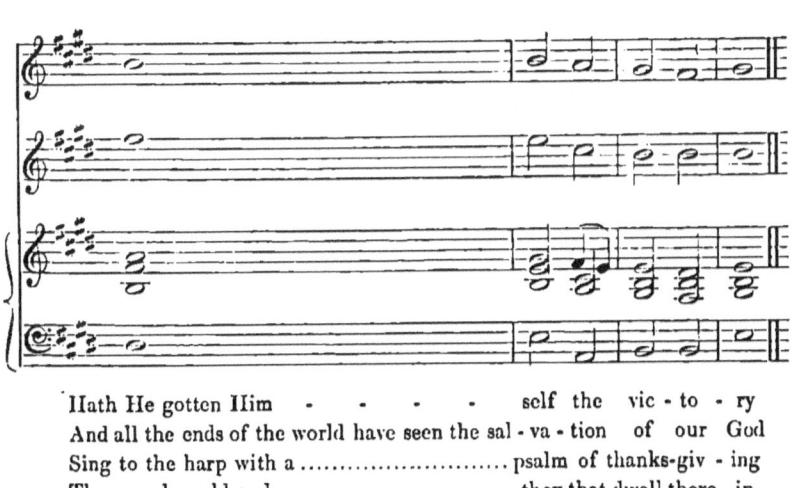

Hath He gotten Him   -   -   -   -   -   self the   vic - to - ry
And all the ends of the world have seen the sal - va - tion   of   our   God
Sing to the harp with a .... psalm of thanks-giv - ing
The round world and .... they that dwell there - in
And the .... people with   e - qui - ty
World .... with - out   end   A - men

No. 47.   CANTATE.   Boyce.

No. 48.   CANTATE.   Dr. Norris.

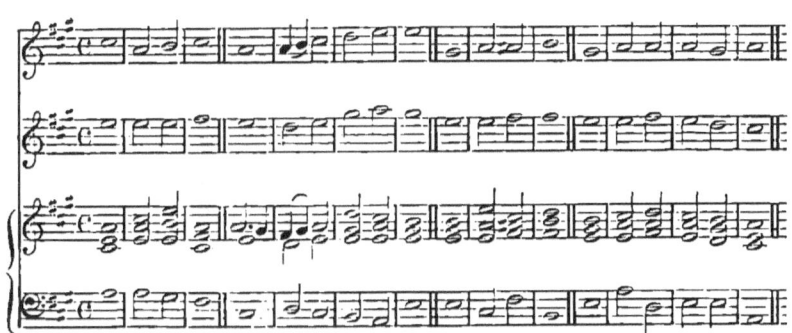

No. 49.   CANTATE.   Dr. Camidge.

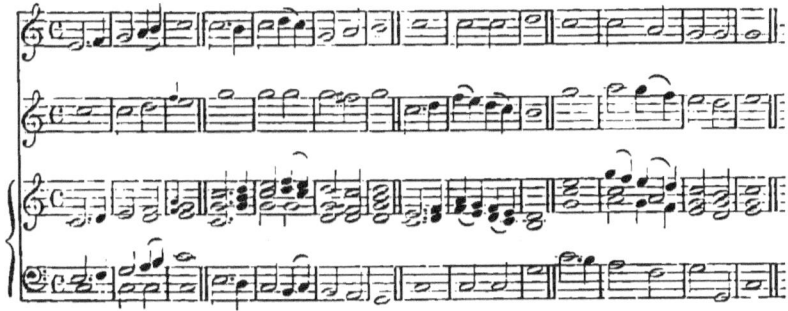

No. 50. CANTATE. GOODENOUGH.

No. 51. CANTATE. Dr Crotch.

No. 52. CANTATE. Entwistle.

No. 53. CANTATE. Beckwith.

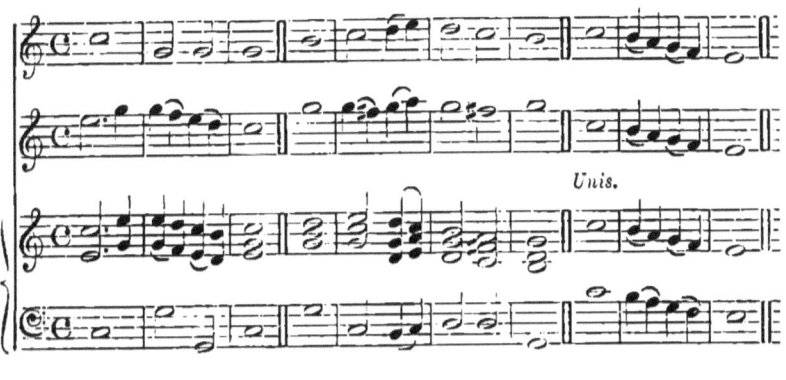

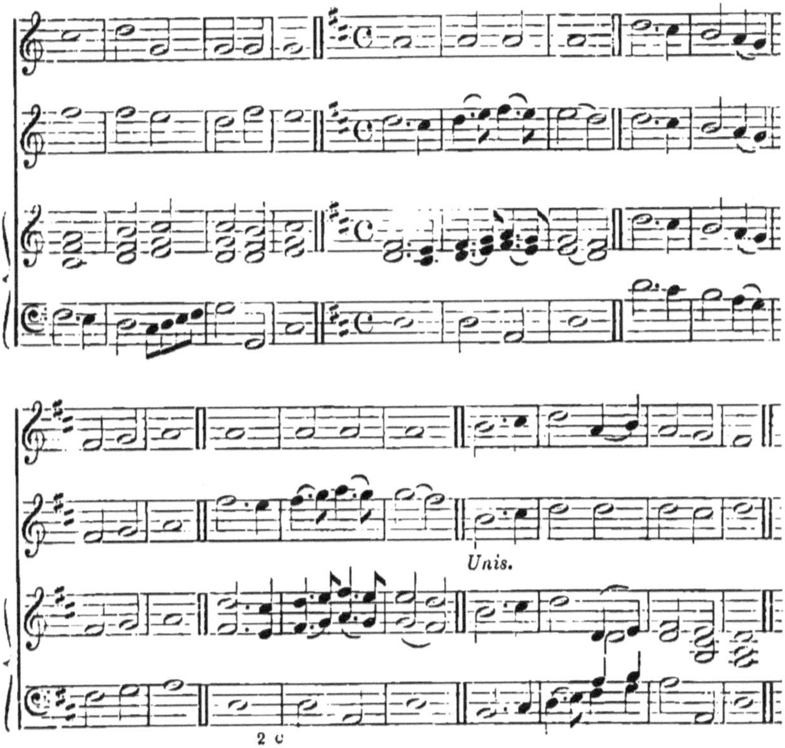

No. 54.   CANTATE.   Eldon.

No. 55. CANTATE.

No. 60.   CANTATE.   MUTLOW.

No. 61.   CANTATE.

HOULDSWORTH.

No. 62. NUNC DIMITTIS.
BATTISHILL.

Lord now lettest thou thy servant de - - - part in peace
Which Thou.. hast pre - pared
Glory be to the Father and........................ to the Son

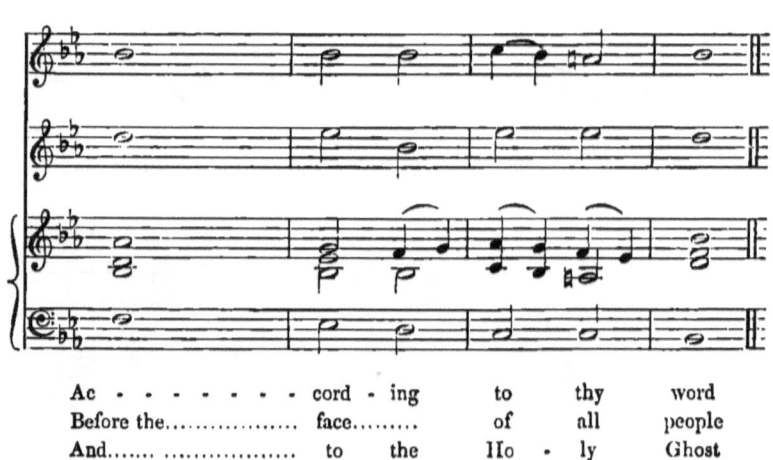

Ac - - - - - - - cord - ing to thy word
Before the................... face......... of all people
And....... .... to the Ho - ly Ghost

For mine..... .... eyes have seen
To be a light to... lighten the gentiles
As it was in the beginning is now and............ ever shall be

Thy... sal - vation
And to be the glory.................. of thy peo - ple Israel
World .... with - out end A - men.

No. 63. NUNC DIMITTIS. Rev. F. D. Sempriere.

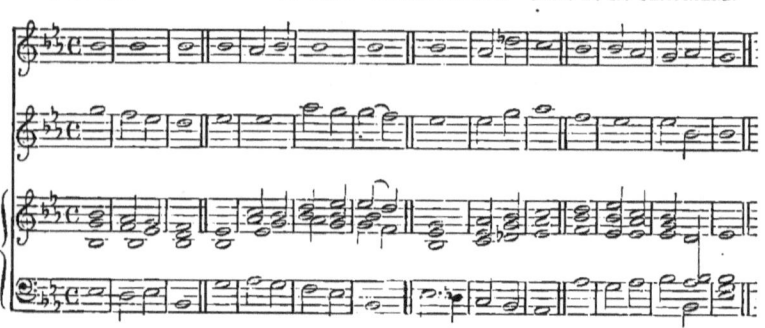

No. 64. NUNC DIMITTIS. Stopford.

No. 65. NUNC DIMITTIS. Vander Meulen.

No. 66.   **NUNC DIMITTIS.**   Dr. Randall.

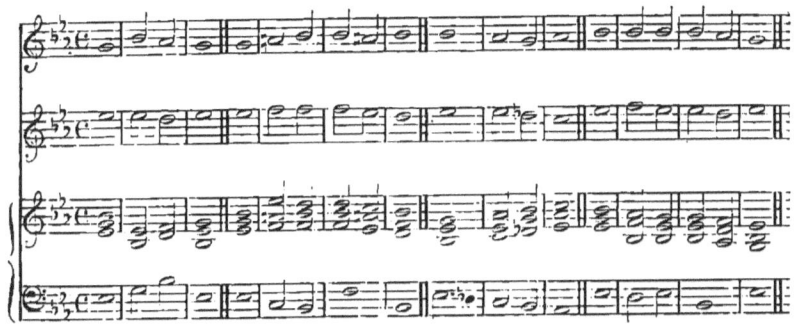

No. 67.   **NUNC DIMITTIS.**   Dr. Hayes.

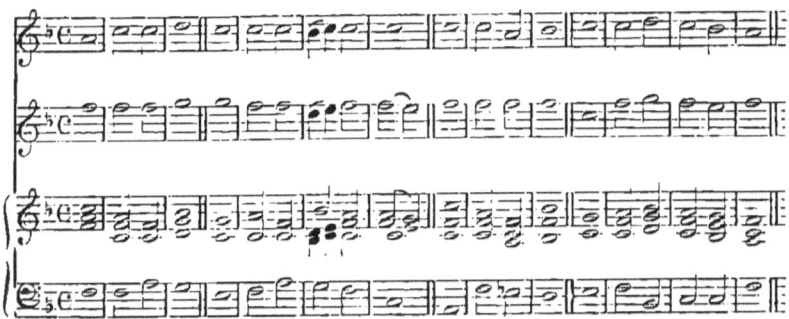

No. 68.   **NUNC DIMITTIS.**   Russell.

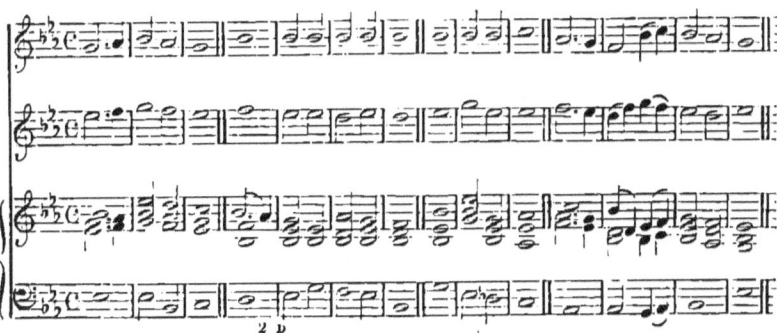

No. 69. NUNC DIMITTIS. JACKSON.

No. 70. NUNC DIMITTIS. HOULDSWORTH.

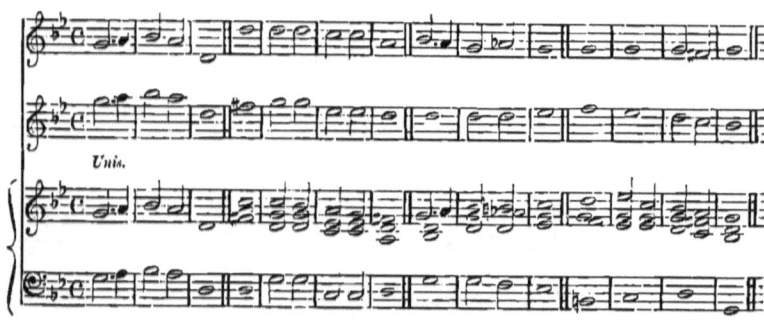

No. 71. NUNC DIMITTIS. SUDLOW.

No. 72.　　　　NUNC DIMITTIS.　　　Beckwith.

No. 73.　　　　NUNC DIMITTIS.　　　Dr. Alcock.

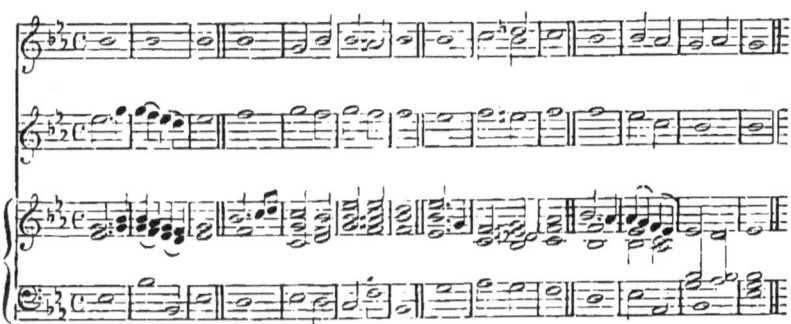

No. 74.　　　　NUNC DIMITTIS.　　　Russell.

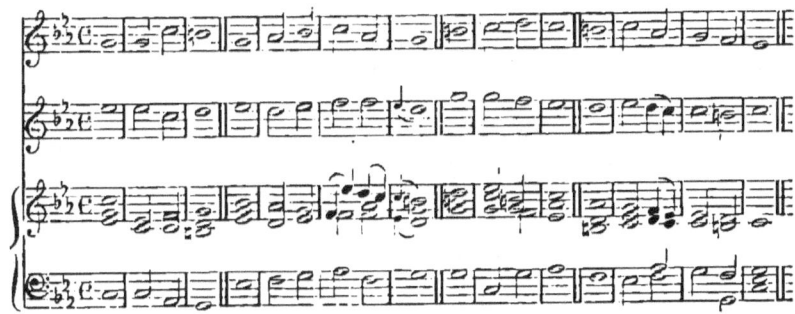

No. 75. NUNC DIMITTIS. Salmon.

No. 76. NUNC DIMITTIS.

No. 77. NUNC DIMITTIS. Felton.

No. 78. NUNC DIMITTIS. Purcell.

No. 79. NUNC DIMITTIS. Dr Croft.

No. 83. MAGNIFICAT. Jones.

My soul doth magni - - - - - - - - fy the Lord

For He............	hath	re - garded
For behold............	from	hence - forth
For He that is mighty hath............	mag	- ni - fied me
And his mercy is on............	them	that fear Him
He hath showed strength............	with	his arm
He hath put down the mighty............	from	their seat
He hath filled the hungry............	with	good things
He remembering his mercy hath holpen his......	ser	- vant Israel
Glory be to the Father and............	to	the Son
As it was in the beginning is now and............	ever	shall be

And my spirit hath re - - - - - - joiced in God my Saviour

The lowliness............	of his	hand-mai - den
All gene - - - - - - - - - -	rations shall	call me blessed
And............	ho - ly	is his name
Throughout............	all gene	- ra - - - tions
He hath scattered the proud in the imagi	- na - tion	of their hearts
And hath ex - - - - - - - - -	alted the	humble and meek
And the rich He............	hath sent	empty a - way
As He promised to our forefathers Abraham and his	seed	for ever
And............	to the	Ho - ly Ghost
World............	with -out	end A - men.

No. 84.   MAGNIFICAT.

No. 85.   MAGNIFICAT.   Hartley.

No. 86.   MAGNIFICAT.   Humphries.

No. 87.   MAGNIFICAT.   Hartley.

No. 88.   MAGNIFICAT.   Dr. Hayes.

No. 89.   MAGNIFICAT.

No. 90.   DEUS MISEREATUR.   JONES.

God be merciful unto............................ us   and   bless us

That thy way may be known........................ up - on   earth
Let the people praise............................... Thee   O   God
O let the nations rejoice............................ and   be   glad
Let the people praise............................... Thee   O   God
Then shall the earth bring forth .... her   in - crease
God... shall   bless   us
Glory be to the Father and .... to   the   Son
As it was in the beginning is now and .... ever   shall   be

And show us the light of his countenance and be mer-ci-ful unto us

Thy saving... health a- mong all nations
Yea let all the...................................... peo-ple praise Thee
For Thou shalt judge the folk righteously and }
  govern the.. na-tions up - on earth
Yea let all the...................................... peo - ple praise Thee
And God even our own God....................... shall give us his blessing
And all the ends of the............................ world shall fear Him
And... to the Ho-ly Ghost
World... with - out end A-men.

206

No. 2. RESPONSE. *Arranged by* J. HOULDSWORTH.

No. 3. RESPONSE.

PRATT.

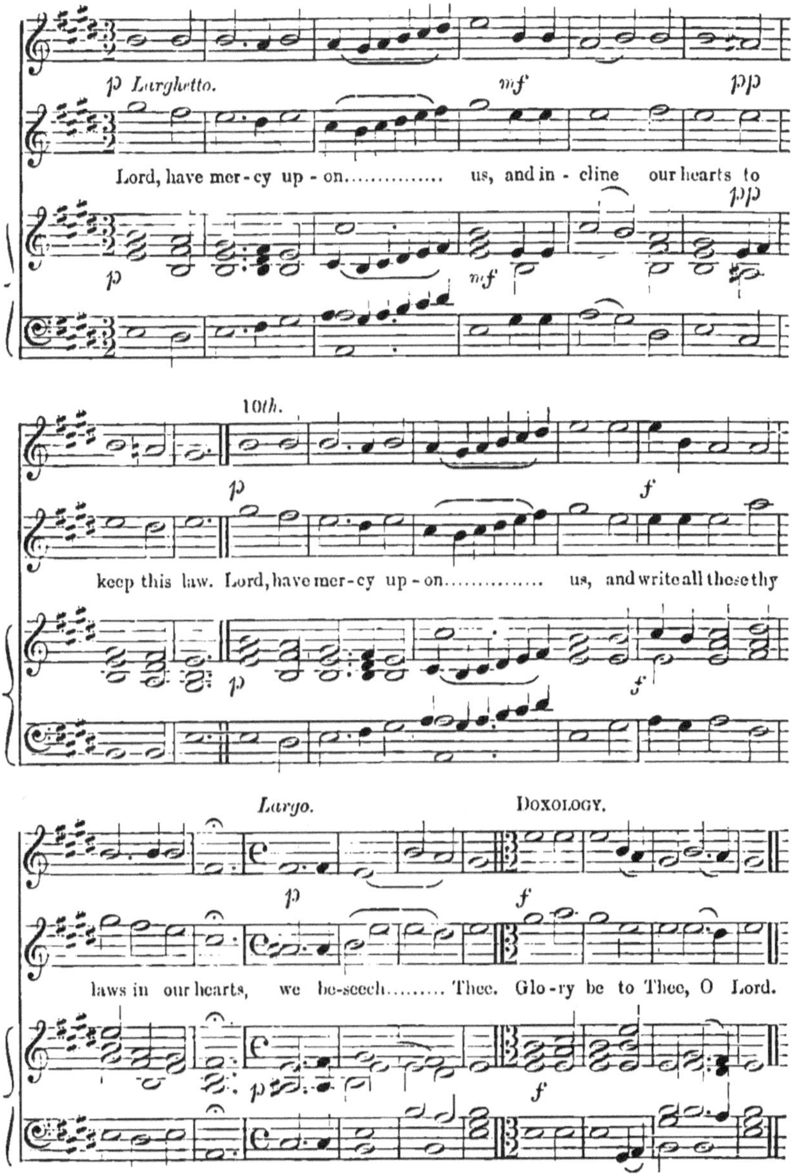
p Larghetto.
mf
pp
Lord, have mer-cy up-on.............. us, and in-cline our hearts to
pp
p
mf
10th.
p
f
keep this law. Lord, have mer-cy up-on.............. us, and write all these thy
p
f
Largo.
DOXOLOGY.
p
f
laws in our hearts, we be-seech......... Thee. Glo-ry be to Thee, O Lord.
p
f

212

No. 8.   RESPONSE.   Jomelli.

214

No. 10.   RESPONSE.   Arranged by J. HOULDSWORTH.

No. 11. RESPONSE. EDDON.

Lord, have mer-cy up - on us, and in - cline our hearts to keep this law. Lord, have mer-cy up - on us, and write all these thy laws in our hearts, we be - seech Thee. Glo - ry be to Thee, O Lord.

214

No. 10.   RESPONSE.   Arranged by
J. HOULDSWORTH.

Lord, have mer-cy up - on us, and in-cline our hearts, and incline our hearts to keep this law. Lord, have mer-cy up - on us, and write all these thy laws in our hearts, we be-seech Thee. Glory be to Thee, O Lord.

No. 11.   RESPONSE.   EDDON.

215

220

No. 16.   RESPONSE.   HOULDSWORTH.

Lord, have mer-cy up-on us, and in-cline our hearts to keep this law. Lord, have mer-cy up-on us, and write all these thy laws in our hearts, we be-seech Thee. Glo-ry be to Thee, O Lord.

Largo.   DOXOLOGY.

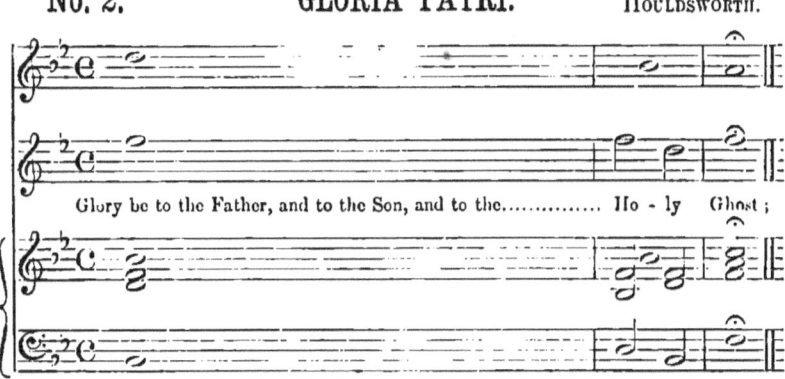

No. 4.   **GLORIA PATRI.**   HOULDSWORTH.

No. 5. GLORIA PATRI. HOULDSWORTH.

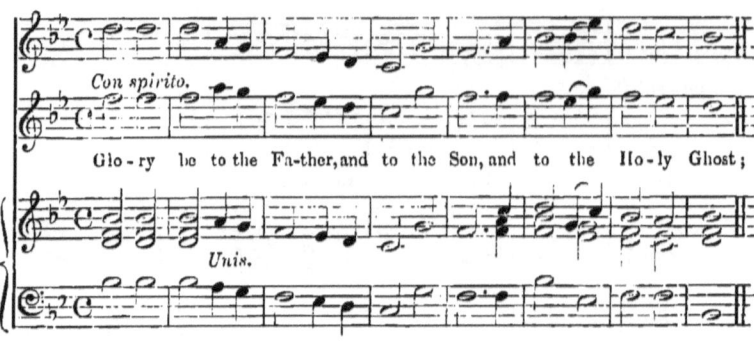

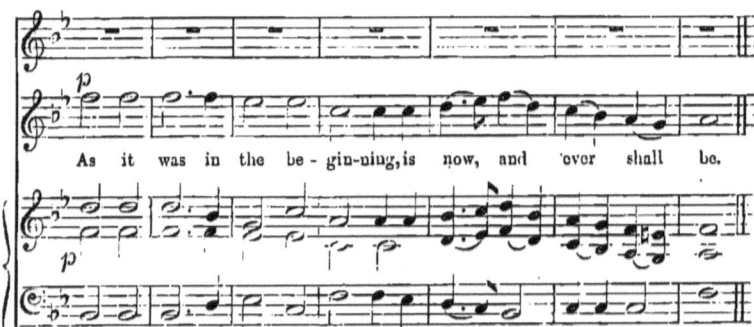

226
No. 7. GLORIA PATRI.
Rev. C. Hoyle.

Glory be to the Father, and to the Son, and to the Ho - ly Ghost;

As it was in the be - ginning, is now, and e - ver shall

callando.

be, World without end, World without end, with-out end, A - men.
Unis.

No. 8. GLORIA PATRI. Houldsworth.

No. 9. GLORIA PATRI. HOULDSWORTH.

Glo-ry be to the Fa - ther, and to the Son, and to the Ho-ly Ghost;

p
As it was in the be - gin-ning, is now, and e-ver shall be,

p
O.

f
A - men.
World without end, :∥: World with-out end. A - men.

f
World without end. A - men, A - men.

229

No. 10. GLORIA PATRI. HOULDSWORTH.

A COLLECT.

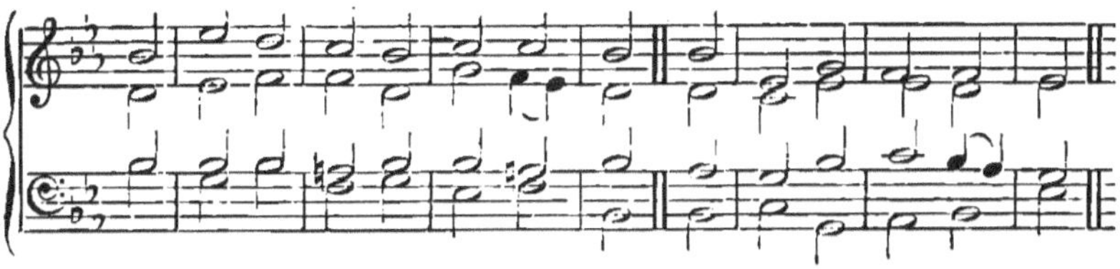

235

No. 6.   CARLISLE. S.M.   LOCKHART.

No. 7.   HALL. 7.7.7.7.   German Melody

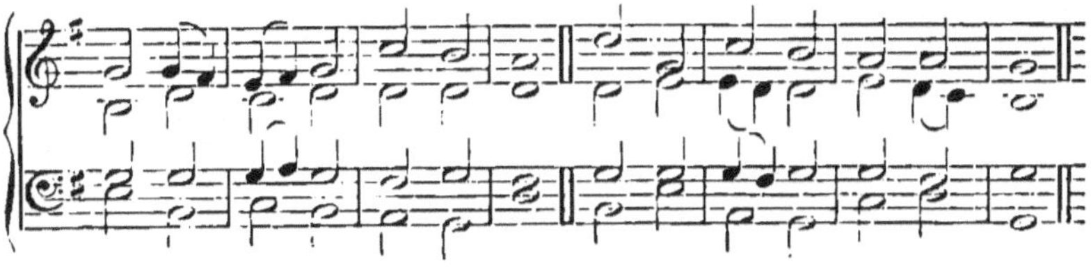

No. 10. " **Weary of earth.** " 10.10.10.10. Dr. Roberts.

Not too slow.

No. 11. S. MICHAEL. S.M. From Day's "Psalter," 1588.

No. 13. "Thou art coming, O my Saviour." 8.7 8.8.7.7.7.7.7.
J. V. Roberts.

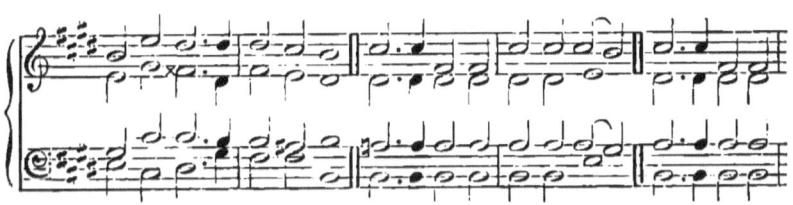
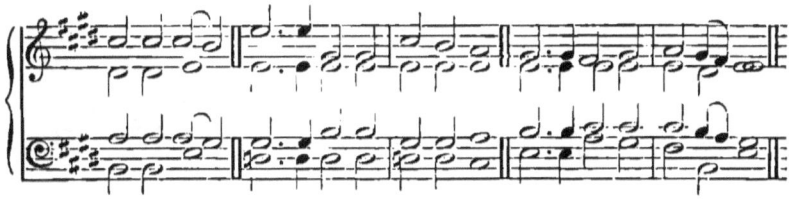

No. 14. WEBER. 7.7.7.7. From WEBER.

No. 15. S. THEODULPH. 7.6.7.6.7.6.7.6. TESCHNER.

241

No. 16.   LUBECK. 7.7.7.7.   German Melody.

No. 17.   SHERBORNE. 7.7.7.7.   From Mendelssohn.

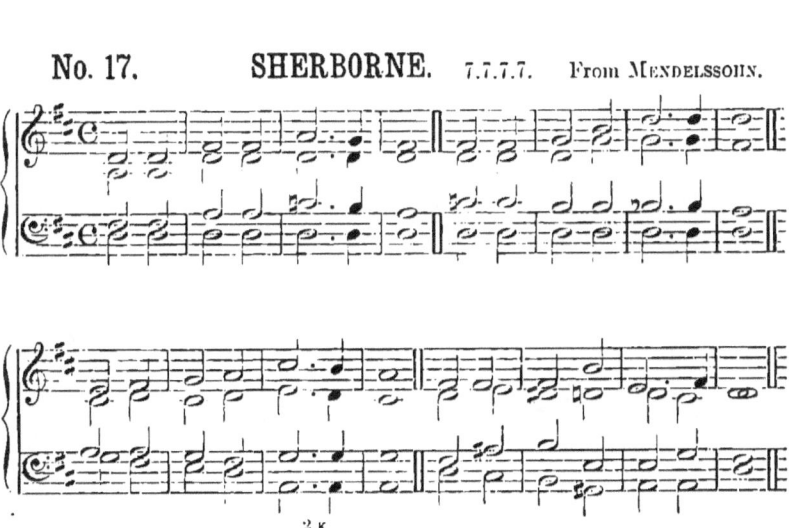

No. 18. VIENNA. 7.7.7.7. German Chorale.

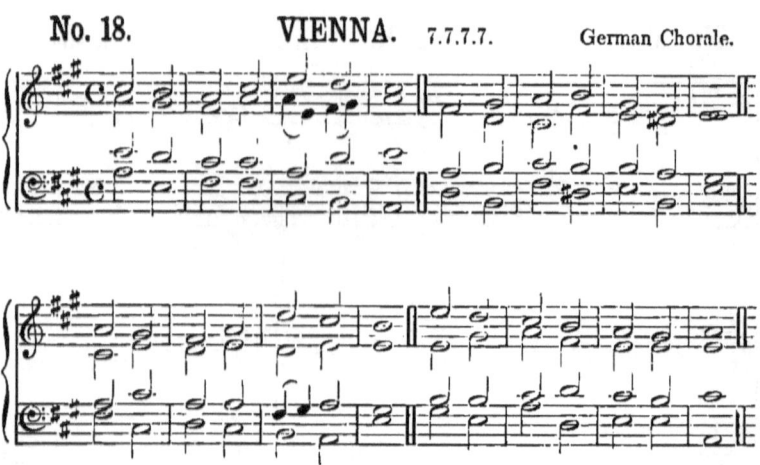

No. 19. DIX. 7.7.7.7.7.7. German.

No. 20.   BATAVIA. 8.7.8.7.   German.

No. 21.   JERSEY. 7.7.7.7.   Dr. Boyce.

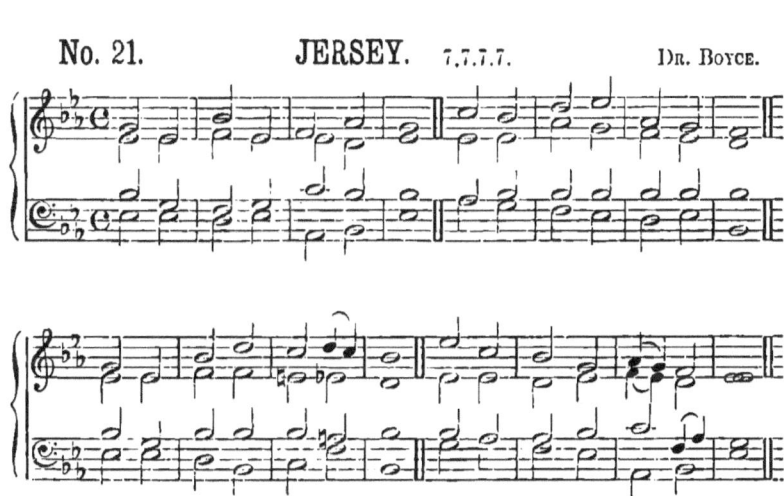

No. 22.   TOULON. 10.10.10.10.   Goudimel.

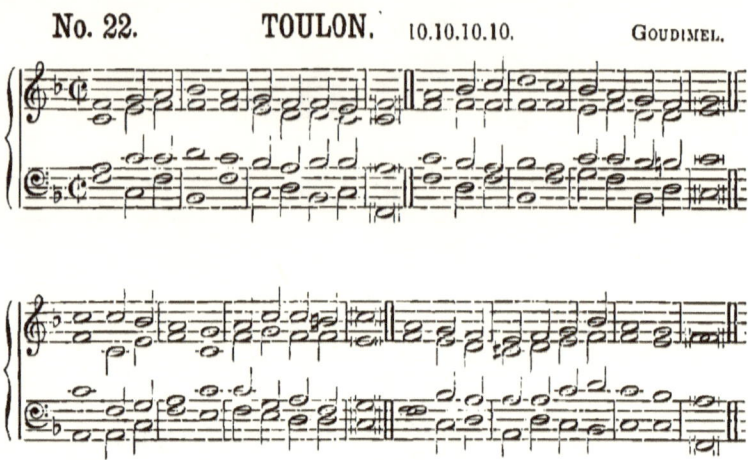

No. 23.   TALLIS. C.M.   Tallis.

No. 24.   ANGEL'S HYMN. L.M.   GIBBONS.

No. 25.   SWABIA. S.M.   German Melody.

No. 26.   AUGUSTINE. S.M.   J. S. BACH.

No. 27.   FARRANT. C.M.   FARRANT.

No. 28. KEBLE. 8.8.8.6. BOOTH SHARP.

No. 29. EVENTIDE. 6.5.6.5. BOOTH SHARP.

261

No. 66.   GARNETT.

No. 67.   P. HAYES.

No. 68.   W. HAYES.

No. 69.   DR. ALCOCK.

No. 70.   DUPUIS.

264

No. 81. Gregorian.

No. 82. Gregorian.

No. 83. Griffiths.

No. 84. Dr. W. Hayes.

No. 85. Ely.

265

No. 86. C. KING.

No. 87. DR. GREENE.

No. 88. W. A. WOOD.

No. 89. W. A. WOOD.

No. 90. W. A. WOOD.

FOR THE TE DEUM.

No. 91. "We praise Thee, O God." BELLAMY.

"Thou art the King of Glory." BATTISHILL.

"We believe that Thou shalt come." PURCELL.

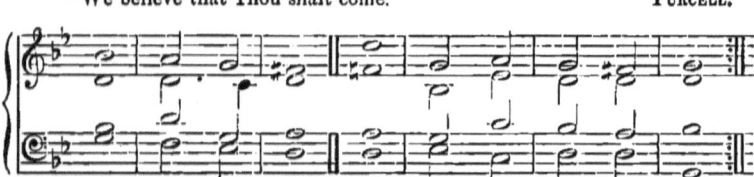

"Day by day." DR. W. HAYES.

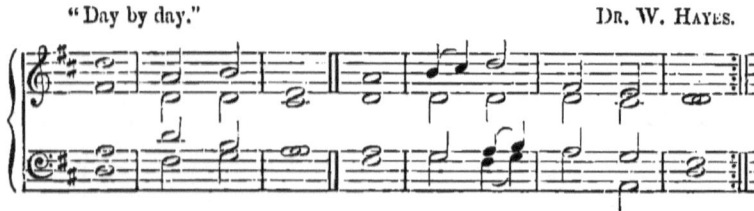

FOR THE TE DEUM.

No. 92. "We praise Thee, O God." GIBBONS.

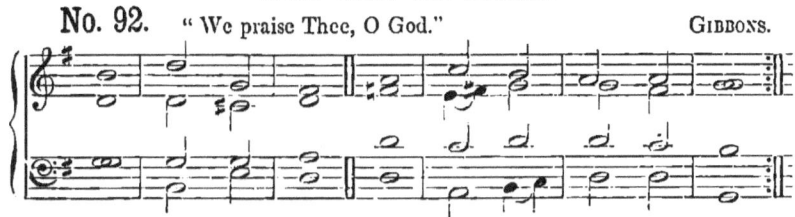

"Thou art the King of Glory." AYLWARD.

"We believe that Thou shalt come." HINE.

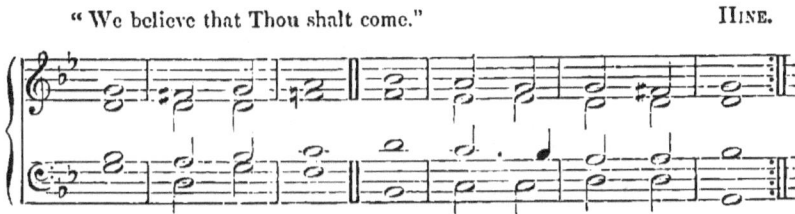

"Day by day." DR. CROTCH.

FOR THE TE DEUM.

No. 93. "We praise Thee, O God." J. V. ROBERTS.

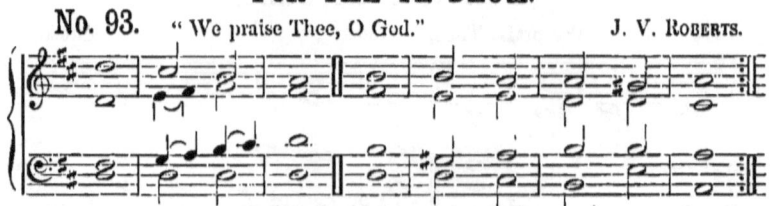

"Thou art the King of Glory." J. V. ROBERTS.

"We believe that Thou shalt come." J. V. ROBERTS.

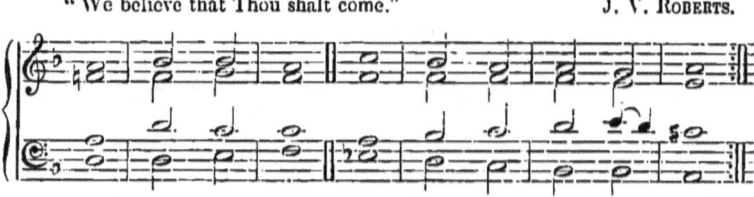

"Day by day." J. V. ROBERTS.

FOR THE TE DEUM.

No. 94. "We praise Thee, O God." Dr. Crotch.

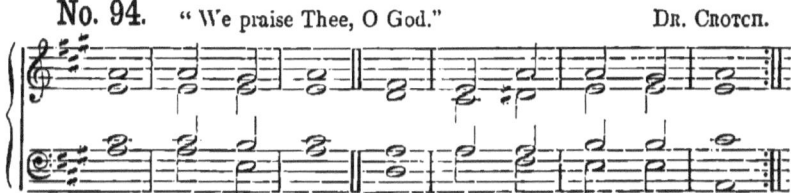

"Thou art the King of Glory." Gregorian.

"We believe that Thou shalt come." Gregorian.

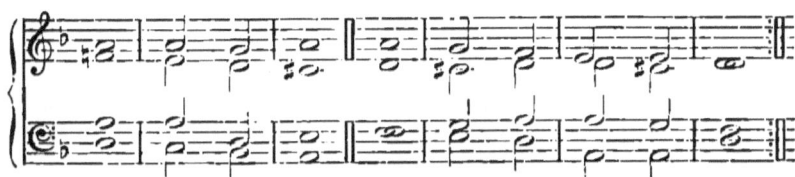

"Day by day." Dr. Alcock.

FOR THE TE DEUM.

No. 95. "We praise Thee, O God." Dr. Alcock.

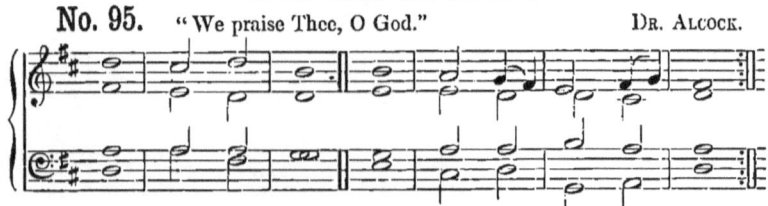

"Thou art the King of Glory." Tucker.

"We believe that Thou shalt come." Haigh.

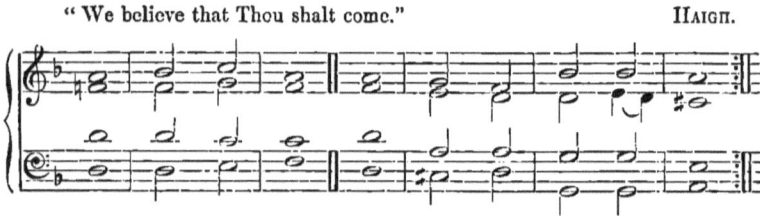

"Day by day."

DOUBLE CHANTS.

No. 1. Dr. Crotch.

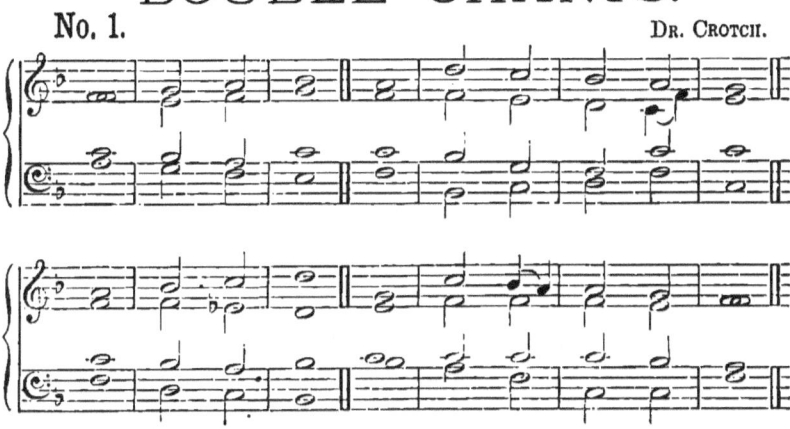

No. 2. Dr. Roberts.

No. 3.
T. S. Dupuis.

No. 4.
T. S. Dupuis.

273

No. 5.　　　　　　　　　　　　　　　　　　　　J. V. Roberts.

No. 6.　　　　　　　　　　　　　　　　　　　　Mornington.

No. 7.
BENNETT.

No. 8.
ROGERS.

No. 9. SOAPER.

No. 10. DR. NARES.

No. 11.
Woodward.

No. 12.
Dr. Crotch.

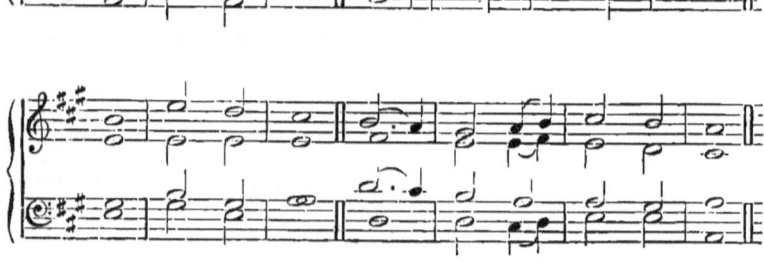

No. 13.
R. Cooke.

No. 14.
Aldrich.

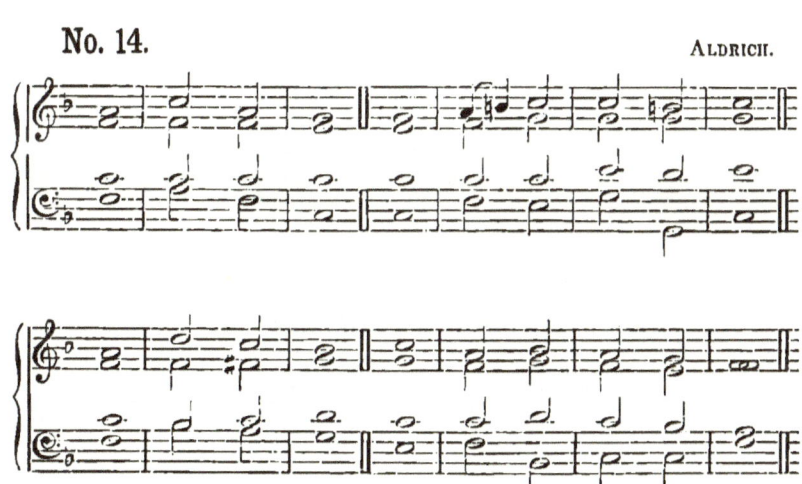

No. 15.
R. Cooke.

No. 16.
Dr. W. Hayes.

No. 17.

ATTWOOD.

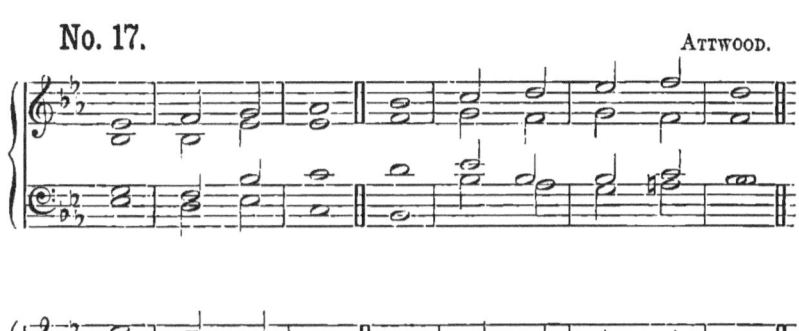

No. 18.

DUPUIS.

No. 19.　　　　　　　　　　　　　　　　　　Lawes.

No. 20.　　　　　　　　　　　　　　　　　　Morley.

No. 21.
HIGGINS.

No. 22.
DR. BOYCE.

THE NICENE CREED IN MONOTONE.

(The words of recitation to be distinctly articulated, as in good chanting; in other places they will fall easily into the indicated measures.)

J. V. ROBERTS, Mus. Doc., Oxon.

www.ingramcontent.com/pod-product-compliance
Lightning Source LLC
Chambersburg PA
CBHW022107230426
43672CB00008B/1313